Presented to

Laura

by

Your godparents Ray & Grandma

on

Christmas 1999 - Laura's first Christmas

*****

All our love & prayers are with you

Concept and editing: Diane Stortz
Special assistance: Andy Rector, Orrin Root,
Jon Underwood
Bible helps: Greg Holder
Design: Coleen Davis

The Standard Publishing Company, Cincinnati, Ohio.
A division of Standex International Corporation.
© 1994, 1998 by The Standard Publishing Company.
All rights reserved.
Printed in the United States of America.
05 04 03 02 01 00 99 98   5 4 3 2 1

Library of Congress Catalog Number 94-065942
ISBN 0-7847-0505-4
RL 2.0

The Young Reader's BIBLE

Stories retold by
Bonnie Bruno and Carol Reinsma
Illustrated by Jenifer Schneider

STANDARD
PUBLISHING
Cincinnati, Ohio

"You must become
like children
if you want to enter
the kingdom of God."
—Jesus

Table of Contents

Who's Who in the Bible?

and where to find stories about them

The Old Testament

6

Moses

Joshua

Gideon

Samson

Ruth

Samuel

David

Solomon

Elijah

Jonah

Shadrach • Meshach • Abedneg

Daniel

Esther

Nehemiah

Jesus

The New Testament

Zechariah • Elizabeth

John the Baptist

Mary • Joseph

The Shepherds

The Wise Men

Jesus, the Son of God

What's in the Old Testament?

The Bible is divided into two parts, the Old Testament and the New Testament.

Even though the Bible has two parts, it really is *one* story. It's the story of God's wonderful plan for all of us.

The Old Testament tells about the beginning of the world. It also tells us the history of God's special people, the Jews. God chose Abraham to be the father of this special people, the nation of Israel. From this nation, God planned to send a Savior to the whole world. For hundreds of years, God's people waited for this special person to be born. They called him *Messiah*, a word that means "God's chosen one."

In the Old Testament, you will find exciting stories that show the love and power of God. Everything you will read about really happened. Every event was part of God's plan to prepare his people for the coming of the Savior.

The Beginning

from Genesis 1 and 2

God is the beginning

of all things.

God made the heavens

and the earth.

The earth was empty and dark,

with water everywhere.

Then God said,

"Let there be light."

And there was!

There was evening and morning.

This was the first day.

14

Next, God put a wide space
above the water.

God called the space *sky*.

This was the second day.

On the third day,

God gathered the water

into its own places.

Now there were seas

and dry ground.

"Let plants grow in the ground,"

God said. And they did!

Then God said,

"Let there be lights in the sky

for day and for night."

God made the sun,

the moon, and the stars.

This was the fourth day.

On the fifth day,

God made fish for the seas.

He made birds for the sky.

On the sixth day, God made

living things for the land.

Then God said,

"Let us make human beings.

Let them rule

over the fish of the sea,

the birds of the air,

and the living things on land."

God made the first human being

from the dust.

The first man was called Adam.

God breathed into Adam

the breath of life.

God looked at all he had made.

It was very good!

On the seventh day, God rested.

He made that day a holy day.

Man and Woman

from Genesis 2

God planted a garden

in a place called Eden.

Trees grew in the garden.

The trees were beautiful,

and some had fruit

that was good for food.

A river watered the garden.

God put Adam in the garden
to take care of it.
"You may eat the fruit
from any tree in the garden
except one," said God.
"If you eat from the tree
of knowing good and evil,
you will die."

God also said,

"It is not good for Adam

to be alone."

So God brought all the birds

and animals to Adam.

Adam gave each one

a name.

But none of these creatures

was the right helper

for Adam.

So God made Adam

fall into a deep sleep.

Then God made a woman

from Adam's rib.

God brought her to Adam.

Adam said,

"Here is someone like me.

Her bones came from my bones.

Her body came from my body.

I will call her *woman*,

because she was taken

out of man."

Evil Enters Eden

from Genesis 3

One day a sneaky snake
came to the woman.
"Did God really tell you
not to eat fruit
from any tree in the garden?"
asked the snake.
"God told us we may eat fruit
from all the trees except one,"
said Eve.
"God told us we will die
if we eat from that tree."

"You will not die,"

said the snake.

"You will be like God.

You will know good and evil."

The fruit on the tree

looked good to eat.

Eve took some and ate it.

Then she gave some to Adam,

and he ate it, too.

Then Adam and Eve saw

that they were naked.

They made coverings

for themselves.

Soon they heard God walking

through the garden.

Quickly, they hid.

"Where are you?" God called.

"Did you eat from the tree?"

"The woman you put here
gave me the fruit," said Adam.

"The snake tricked me,
and I ate it," said Eve.

"From now on you will crawl
on your belly," God told the snake.

Then God made clothes

for Adam and Eve.

Sadly, he sent them

out of the garden.

"Your work will cause you pain,"

God said.

"And when you die,

your body will turn back to dust."

31

Water, Water Everywhere

from Genesis 6 — 9

Soon many people lived on earth.

But everywhere God looked,

people were sinning.

Only Noah loved God.

"I am going to send a big flood,"

God told Noah.

"Water will cover the whole earth.

Every living thing will die."

Noah listened carefully.

"I want you to build an ark,"

said God. Noah obeyed God.

Two of every kind of animal came to Noah to live on the ark. Then Noah and his family went inside. God closed the door, and the rain began. God sent rain for 40 days.

Water covered the whole world.

Then Noah sent out a dove

to look for dry land.

And one day,

the dove did not come back.

"It is time to go out now!"

called Noah.

Noah and his family

thanked God

for keeping them safe.

God was pleased.

He put a beautiful rainbow

in the sky.

"This is a sign of my promise,"

said God. "I will never send

another flood like this one."

A Surprise for Sarah

from Genesis 12, 15, 18, and 21

God told Abraham

to leave his country.

"I will bless you in a new land,"

God said. Abraham obeyed.

He took his wife, his servants,

and his flocks.

"Can you count the stars?"

God asked Abraham.

There were too many to count!

"So shall your family be,"

said God.

"But I have no children,"

said Abraham.

"Don't worry," said God.

"I will give you a son."

One day, God sent three visitors.

"Please rest under my tree,"

said Abraham.

"Where is Sarah, your wife?"

asked one visitor.

"In the tent," said Abraham.

"Sarah is going to have a son,"

said the visitor.

Sarah heard the news.

She laughed to herself.

"Abraham and I are too old

to have a baby," she said.

The visitor knew

that Sarah laughed.

"Is anything too hard for God?"

he said.

God kept his promise.

The next year,

baby Isaac was born!

Abraham was 100

when he held

his newborn son.

Sarah laughed out loud
this time.
"Everyone who hears about this
will be happy for us!"
she said.

A Very Hairy Trick

from Genesis 25, 27, and 28

God gave twin boys

to Isaac and his wife, Rebekah.

Esau grew up to be a hunter.

Jacob liked to do quiet work

at home around the tents.

By then, Isaac was very old.

It was time for him

to give his blessing to Esau,

his firstborn son.

44

But Rebekah

planned a trick.

Rebekah cooked
Isaac's favorite meal.
"Put on Esau's clothes,"
she told Jacob.
"Put these animal skins
on your hands and neck.
Now take this food
to your father."

Isaac was blind,

but he held Jacob's hands

and felt the hairy skins.

He smelled Esau's clothes.

The trick worked. After Isaac ate,

he gave his blessing to Jacob.

47

Esau also brought food to Isaac.

"Give me your blessing now,"

he said.

Then Isaac knew

he had been tricked.

Esau was sad and angry.

"My own brother

has stolen my blessing!" he cried.

Rebekah was afraid.

"Esau may hurt you,"

she told Jacob. "You must leave."

So Jacob left home to live

with his uncle in another land.

A Pillow and a Promise

from Genesis 28, 32, and 33

On his way to see his uncle,

Jacob stopped to sleep.

He used a stone for a pillow.

While Jacob slept,

God sent him a special dream.

50

In his dream, Jacob saw angels
going up and down
a tall ladder.
The ladder led to heaven.
At the top stood God.

God spoke to Jacob

in the dream.

"I am the God of Abraham

and the God of Isaac," he said.

"I will give this land to you

and all your children.

The whole world

will be blessed

through your family.

I am with you always,"

said God.

"You do not need

to be afraid."

Jacob woke up.

"Surely God is in this place!"

he said. In the morning,

Jacob took his stone pillow

and set it up as a pillar.

He poured oil over it.

Many years passed.

Jacob began a trip home

to see his father, Isaac.

But Jacob was still afraid

of his brother.

Jacob sent Esau a message.

And Jacob asked God for help.

Jacob bowed down

when he saw Esau.

But Esau ran with open **arms**

to meet his brother.

The brothers hugged

and cried happy tears.

Jacob gave Esau a **present**.

It felt good to be going **home**!

Sold! A Sneaky Deal

from Genesis 35 and 37

Jacob had 12 sons,

but he loved Joseph the most.

Jacob gave Joseph

a wonderful coat.

Joseph's brothers were jealous.

56

"Listen to my dreams,"
said Joseph.
"In the field, my bundle of grain
stood up straight. Your bundles
bowed down to mine.
Then I dreamed
the sun and the moon
and 11 stars bowed to me."

"Do you think

we will bow down to you?"

said Joseph's brothers.

They were angry.

One day Joseph went to see

his brothers in the field.

"Here comes that dreamer,"

said the brothers.

"Let's get rid of him."

Joseph's brothers tore off

his wonderful coat.

They threw him into a pit.

"Look," said a brother.

"A group of traders.

Let's sell Joseph to them!"

59

The traders took Joseph.

Then the brothers dipped

Joseph's coat in goat's blood.

They took the coat to their father.

"Is this Joseph's coat?"

they asked him.

"It is!" cried Jacob.

"A wild animal

must have killed him."

Jacob cried for many days.

No one could comfort him.

Meanwhile, Joseph became a slave

in Egypt.

Double Dreams

from Genesis 39 — 41

In Egypt,

Joseph was put into prison

for something he did not do.

The king's cupbearer

was put into prison, too.

One morning,

the cupbearer said,

"I had a strange dream last night.

What does it mean?"

"God knows," said Joseph.

Joseph told the cupbearer

the meaning of his dream.

In three days,

the dream came true.

The cupbearer was called back

to the palace.

"Remember me," said Joseph.

But the cupbearer forgot.

Two years later, Pharaoh the king

had strange dreams.

The cupbearer

remembered Joseph.

"I know a man who can tell

the meaning of dreams,"

said the cupbearer.

"Send for him," said Pharaoh.

Pharaoh told Joseph his dreams.

"I saw seven fat cows," he said.

"Seven skinny cows ate them up.

Then seven thin heads of grain

ate up seven full heads."

"God gave you two dreams
that mean the same thing,"
said Joseph.
"There will be seven good years
with plenty of food.
Then there will be
seven bad years with nothing."
"God has made you wise,"
said Pharaoh. "I will put you
in charge of the land."

For seven years,

Joseph saved grain in barns.

Then the bad years came.

But there was food in Egypt

because Joseph had saved it up.

God Meant It for Good

from Genesis 42 — 47

Joseph's brothers went to Egypt

to buy grain.

They saw Joseph there,

but they did not know him.

I will find out if my brothers

have changed, thought Joseph.

"You are spies," he said.

"No," said the brothers.

"We are honest men.

Our father and our brother

Benjamin are at home."

"Prove that you are honest,"

said Joseph.

"Go now. Come back

with your brother Benjamin."

The brothers went home.

When their grain was gone,

they came back to Egypt

with Benjamin.

This time, Joseph told his servant

to hide a silver cup

in Benjamin's bag.

In the morning, Joseph sent
his servant after the brother.
The silver cup was found
in Benjamin's bag.
"Make us your slaves,
not Benjamin!" cried the brothers.
Joseph saw that his brothers
had changed.

"Come close to me," Joseph said.

"I am your brother Joseph."

The brothers shook with fear.

"Don't be upset," said Joseph.

"You wanted to hurt me.

But God meant it for good.

God used me to save you.

Go and bring our father here."

In a dream, God promised Jacob

that his family

would become great

in Pharaoh's land.

So Jacob and all his family

went to live in Egypt.

Baby Moses' Riverboat

from Exodus 1 and 2

Jacob's family, the Hebrews, grew.

"There are too many Hebrews

in Egypt," said a new pharaoh.

Pharaoh made the Hebrews slaves,

because he was afraid of them.

Pharaoh also made a law.
All new Hebrew baby boys
must be killed.
But one Hebrew mother
hid her baby in a basket.
She floated the basket
at the edge of the river.

The princess of Egypt
found the little baby.
"This is a Hebrew baby,"
she said softly.
The baby's sister was watching.
She ran to the princess.
"Shall I find a Hebrew woman

to nurse the baby for you?"

"Yes, please do,"

said the princess.

The girl came back

with the baby's own mother!

Surely God is watching over

this baby, the mother thought.

The baby's mother
took him home
and cared for him.
When he was older,
his mother took him
to the princess.
The princess adopted him
as her own son.
"I will call him Moses,"
she said,
"because I took him
out of water."

I Am Sending You

from Exodus 2 — 4

In Egypt, the Hebrews

were also called Israelites.

Years earlier,

God had changed Jacob's name

to Israel. The Israelites

were slaves in Egypt a long time.

But God had a plan for them.

Moses grew up. He left Egypt
and became a shepherd.
In the desert near a mountain,
Moses saw a bush on fire.
"How strange," said Moses.
"The bush is on fire,
but it is not burning up!"

Then God called to Moses

from the bush.

Moses covered his face

because he was afraid

to look at God.

"I have heard the cries

of my people," said God.

"And I am sending you

to bring them out of Egypt."

"But God, why me?" said Moses.

"I will be with you," said God.

"But what if no one listens
to me?" cried Moses.

"Throw your staff down,"
said God.

The staff became a snake.

"Now pick it up," said God.

The snake became a staff again.

"Show this
to the people,"
said God.

"But I am not a good speaker,"

said Moses.

"Your brother Aaron

will go with you and help you,"

God said.

Then Moses started back to Egypt.

And God sent Aaron

to meet Moses in the desert.

Ten Terrible Troubles

from Exodus 5 — 12

Moses and Aaron told Pharaoh,

"God says, Let my people

go into the desert to worship me."

"No!" said Pharaoh.

"Why should I obey your God?"

"Go back to Pharaoh," God said.

"Tell Aaron to throw down

his staff."

Aaron's staff became a snake.

"My magicians can do that, too,"

said Pharaoh.

Aaron's staff swallowed

the staffs of the magicians.

But Pharaoh still would not

let God's people go.

Then God sent troubles
on the Egyptians.
First the water turned to blood.
Then frogs covered the land.
Dust turned into biting gnats.
Flies swarmed everywhere.
All of Egypt's livestock died.
Egypt's people broke out in boils.
Hail killed people, plants,
and animals.
Hungry locusts ate the crops.
Darkness covered Egypt
for three days.

But stubborn Pharaoh still
would not let God's people go.

89

Then God told Moses,

"Every firstborn in Egypt will die.

Even Pharaoh's firstborn.

Tell my people to roast lamb

for their last meal in Egypt.

Tell them to smear the blood of

the lamb on their doorframes."

The Israelites obeyed God.

That night the firstborn

of every Egyptian family died.

But no one died in a house

with blood on the doorframe.

"Take your people and flocks,

and go!" Pharaoh cried to Moses.

Pharaoh's Biggest Mistake

from Exodus 12 — 15

The Israelites were free!

God led them along a desert road.

During the day,

God went ahead of them

in a pillar of cloud.

At night, God went ahead of them

in a pillar of fire.

But in Egypt, Pharaoh was sorry

he had let God's people go.

"Who will work for me now?"

he said. "We must bring

those people back!"

The Israelites were camped
beside the Red Sea.
They screamed when they saw
Pharaoh and his chariots.
But Moses said, "Don't be afraid!
The Lord will fight for you."
The tall cloud moved
between the Israelites
and the soldiers.
Then Moses raised his staff
and pointed it toward the sea.
God sent a mighty wind
to part the water.

94

All night long, the Israelites crossed the Red Sea on dry land while God held back the water.

Pharaoh's army tried to follow

the Israelites. But God told Moses,

"Lift your staff again."

Moses obeyed.

The water of the sea

flowed back into place.

All of Pharaoh's soldiers drowned.

But God's people were safe

on the other side of the sea.

Moses and the Israelites

sang a song of praise to God.

Moses' sister, Miriam,

led the women in a dance.

The Israelites were ready

to follow God anywhere.

A Special Treasure

from Exodus 16, 17, 19, 20, and 31

In the wilderness,

the Israelites became hungry

and thirsty.

But God covered the ground

with *manna* bread every morning

and sometimes quail for meat.

98

"Hit that rock with your staff,"

God told Moses.

Water poured from the rock!

The people camped by a mountain.
Moses went up the mountain
to talk to God.
"Tell my people to obey me,"
God said. "Then they
will be my special
treasure."

Moses gave God's message
to the people. After three days,
he led them out of the camp
to the mountain. Thick smoke
covered the mountain
because God was there.

God spoke to the people.

He gave them ten commandments.

1. Have no other gods but me.

2. Do not worship idols.

3. Use my name for good.

4. Keep the seventh day a holy day.

5. Love and honor your parents.

6. Do not murder.

7. Be true to your husband or wife.

8. Never take what is not yours.

9. Always be honest.

10. Do not be jealous of what others have.

Then Moses went up
on the mountain again.
God gave him
the ten commandments
on two stone tablets.

Faith or Fear?

from Numbers 13 and 14

God told Moses

to send 12 men

to explore the land of Canaan.

"I will give this land

to my people," said God.

"See what the people are like,"

Moses told the 12 men.

"See what their towns are like."

After 40 days,

the men came back.

"The land is flowing

with milk and honey," they said.

"Here is its fruit.

But the people are strong,

and their cities have walls."

Caleb said,

"We should not be afraid.

We can take the land."

But other men said,

"The people are stronger

than we are.

We can't fight them and win."

God's people grumbled to Moses.

"It would be better

if we went back to Egypt,"

they said.

Then Caleb and Joshua

stood before the people.

"The Lord will lead us

into the land," Joshua said.

"He will give it to us."

But the people talked about

killing Joshua and Caleb.

God was angry

with his people.

"You will live and die
here in the desert," God said.
So it was 40 years
before the people
went into the land of Canaan,
the land God had promised them.

Seven Times and a Shout

from Joshua 5 and 6

The gates of Jericho
were shut tight.
No one went out or in.
Then the angel of the Lord
came to Joshua.

"What does God want to tell me?"

Joshua asked the angel.

"I have given you this city,"

was God's answer.

"Here is what you must do.

March your army

around the city.

Do it once a day for six days.

Carry the stone tablets

with the ten commandments

in their special box.

Have seven priests

blow trumpets as you march."

God told Joshua

that the battle would be won

on the seventh day.

"March around the city

seven times on that day,"

said God. "On the seventh time,

shout,

and the walls will fall down."

Joshua obeyed God.

With the army and the priests,

he marched around the city

of Jericho.

Early the next morning,

Joshua and the army

and the priests marched again.

They did this for six days.

On the seventh day,

they marched seven times

around the city.

On the seventh time,

Joshua called out, "Shout!

For the Lord has given you

the city."

The priests gave a loud blast

on the trumpets.

The people shouted.

With a crash, the walls of Jericho

fell to the ground!

Torches and Trumpets

from Judges 6 and 7

After many years in Canaan,

the Israelites stopped obeying God.

So God allowed

the people of Midian

to take over the land.

The Israelites had to live in caves.

Finally, they asked God for help.

God sent an angel to Gideon,

who was threshing wheat.

"The Lord is with you,"

the angel said.

"Go and save Israel from Midian."

"Lord," said Gideon,

"I will put out

a piece of wool tonight.

In the morning, let me find dew

on the wool

but not on the ground.

Then I will know

that you will save Israel."

The next morning,

the wool was wet,

but the ground was dry.

"Give me one more sign,"

said Gideon.

The next morning,

the wool was dry,

but the ground was wet.

God gave Gideon a small army
of 300 men.
Each man had a trumpet
and a clay jar with a torch inside.
At night, the army made a circle
around the camp of Midian.
The army blew their trumpets

and smashed their jars.

They shouted,

"A sword for the Lord

and for Gideon!"

The noise and the torches

scared the people of Midian.

They ran as fast as they could go.

Strong Samson

from Judges 13, 15, and 16

Again the Israelites

stopped obeying God.

So God allowed the Philistines

to rule over Israel for 40 years.

Then God sent Samson.

God had said that Samson

should never cut his hair.

For a long time, Samson never did.

Samson was strong.

He fought a thousand Philistines, and won.

He carried away a whole city gate!

Samson met Delilah

and fell in love with her.

The Philistines came to Delilah.

"Find out the secret

of Samson's strength,"

they said.

"We will pay you well."

Day after day,

Delilah asked Samson

to tell her his secret.

Finally Samson said,

"If my hair were cut,

I would lose my strength."

Some Philistines hid
in Delilah's house.
They cut Samson's hair
as he slept.
Then Samson's strength was gone.
The Philistines caught him.

The Philistine kings

held a party

in the temple

of one of their gods.

They made fun of Samson.

Samson prayed,

"Lord, give me strength

one more time."

He pushed against the pillars

that held up the temple.

The temple crashed down.

Many Philistines died,

and Samson died with them.

Ruth's Rich Reward

from the Book of Ruth

No rain fell. No wheat grew.

There was no food in Judah.

Elimelech and his wife, Naomi,

and their two sons

moved to the land of Moab,

where there was food.

The two sons married two women

from Moab.

Their names were Ruth and Orpah.

Later, Elimelech and his sons died.

Naomi, Ruth, and Orpah

were left alone.

News came

that there was food again

in Judah.

Naomi made plans

to go home.

"Let me go with you,"

said Ruth.

"Your people

will be my people.

And your God will be my God."

So Ruth left Moab

and went to Bethlehem in Judah

with Naomi.

When they came to Bethlehem,

Naomi and Ruth were poor.

But God's law

allowed poor people

to pick up fallen grain.

Ruth gathered grain in a field

that belonged to a man

named Boaz.

Ruth was kind to Boaz.

He saw that Ruth was special.

He made plans to marry her.

Ruth became Boaz's wife,

and they had a son, named Obed.

When Obed was old,

he became the grandfather

of the great King David.

A Voice in the Dark

from 1 Samuel 1 — 3

At the tent of worship,

Hannah prayed.

"Give me a son, God," she said.

"I will let him serve you

all his life."

Eli the priest

saw Hannah praying.

"Go home and do not worry,"

said Eli.

God gave Hannah a baby boy!

She named him Samuel.

When Samuel was old enough,

Hannah took him to Eli.

"I am the one who asked God

for a son," she said.

"Now I am giving him

back to God."

Then Samuel lived with Eli,

and Hannah came to visit him.

In the dark one night,

Samuel heard a voice.

"Samuel!" called the voice.

Samuel ran to Eli's room.

"Here I am," said Samuel.

"I did not call you," said Eli.

"Go back to bed."

The voice called to Samuel
three times.
"It is the Lord," said Eli.
"If he calls you again, say,
I am your servant,
and I am listening."

God called Samuel again.

"I am your servant,

and I am listening," said Samuel.

God gave Samuel

a message for Eli.

As Samuel grew up,

God had more messages for him.

Everyone in Israel knew

that Samuel was God's prophet.

A New King for Israel

from 1 Samuel 15 and 16

King Saul of Israel

was not obeying God.

So God told Samuel,

"Go to Bethlehem.

Find the man named Jesse.

I have chosen

one of Jesse's sons

to be the next king."

140

Samuel went to Bethlehem.

He found Jesse and his sons.

One son was very handsome.

He must be

the one God has chosen,

thought Samuel.

But God told Samuel, "No."

Seven sons stepped forward.

Seven times God said,

"This is not the one."

"Do you have any more sons?"

Samuel asked Jesse.

"Yes," said Jesse.

"David is tending the sheep."

Jesse sent for David.

When David came,

God told Samuel,

"This is the one I have chosen.

Anoint him with oil."

After this, an evil spirit

began to bother King Saul.

The king's helpers said,

"Music can help you feel better.

A young man named David

plays the harp."

"Send for him," said King Saul.

David played his harp for Saul.

The music helped the king.

Saul asked Jesse

to let David live in the palace.

He did not know that someday

David would be king!

A Giant Problem

from 1 Samuel 17

Goliath the Philistine

was nine feet tall!

Every day for 40 days,

Goliath waved his spear

and shouted,

"Which of you will fight me?"

The Israelites were afraid.

No one would fight Goliath.

146

David's brothers were soldiers
in Israel's army.
When David came to visit them,
he saw Goliath
and heard his shouts.

"I am not afraid of Goliath,"

said David.

"I will go and fight him."

"You are just a boy,"

said King Saul.

"God helped me protect my sheep

from a lion and a bear,"

said David.

"God will save me from Goliath."

King Saul gave David

his own armor.

"At least wear this," said Saul.

David took the armor off.

"I am not used to it," he said.

David put five smooth stones

in his shepherd's bag.

He carried his staff

and his sling.

"God will give you over

to me today!"

he shouted to Goliath.

David aimed his sling carefully.

With one stone,

he struck Goliath in the forehead.

Goliath fell to the ground

with a crash!

The Philistines ran the other way.

And King Saul's army cheered.

The King Who Sang Praises

from 2 Samuel 2 and 5 and Psalms

David became king

when Saul died.

David loved to worship God

with songs.

He wrote many songs himself.

One of David's songs
tells how God is like
a loving shepherd.

The Lord gives me
everything I need.
I will not be afraid
because
he always protects me.
Goodness and love
will always follow me.

Psalm 23

Another song tells about

God's wonderful creation.

The whole world
belongs to the Lord!
Everything and
everyone are his.
They who seek God
are blessed,
for he is the mighty one.

Psalm 24

Sometimes David told God
about his feelings.

Look at me and be kind to me.
I am lonely and upset.
I am worried about my problems.
Protect and save me.
I am trusting you.

Psalm 25

One of David's songs is about
God's wonderful forgiveness.

I confessed my sin
and you forgave me.
You have given happiness
and peace back to me!
You are full of love, kindness,
and forgiveness.

Psalm 32

Another song praises God
for knowing David so well.

You watch over me
every minute of the day.
You know when I sleep
and when I wake up.
You know what I am thinking.
Anywhere I go
you are there.
You even knew me
before I was born!

Psalm 139

Solomon's One Wish

from 1 Kings 2 — 8

When David died,

his son Solomon became king.

God spoke to Solomon

in a dream.

"Ask me for whatever you want,"

God said.

Solomon asked for only one thing.

"I need wisdom

to be a good king," he said.

God was pleased

with Solomon's prayer.

He made Solomon

the wisest man who ever lived.

People from all nations

came to listen to King Solomon.

God gave Israel a time of peace.
"Now we can build a temple
where we can worship the Lord,"
said Solomon.
Thousands of men cut fine stone
and cedar wood for the temple.

Artists carved pictures
on the walls.
The inside of the temple
was covered with gold.
In seven years,
the temple was finished.
The people of Israel
came to the temple
to celebrate.
Solomon prayed with them.
Then Solomon said,
"Let us promise to always obey
the Lord our God."

Meals for the Messenger

from 1 Kings 16 and 17

King Ahab did more evil

than any king of Israel

before him.

Ahab married Jezebel,

who worshiped an idol

called Baal.

Ahab set up a place

for the people to worship Baal

instead of God.

God sent his prophet Elijah

to King Ahab.

"This is a message

from the Lord,"

Elijah told the king.

"There will be no rain or dew

in Israel until I say so."

Ahab wanted to kill Elijah
because of this news from God.
But God told Elijah,
"Leave here, go east, and hide.
You will drink from the stream.
And I have told the ravens
to bring you bread and meat."

Elijah obeyed God.

He hurried to a hiding place
and stayed there.

He drank water from the stream.

Every morning and every night,
ravens brought bread and meat
to Elijah,
just as God had said.

The Lord, He Is God!

from 1 Kings 18

For three years, there was no rain.

Crops did not grow.

Then God told Elijah,

"Go to King Ahab again.

Soon I will send rain on the land."

When Ahab saw Elijah, he said,

"You are a troublemaker."

170

"Trouble came

because you did not obey God,"

Elijah said.

"Now call the people

to meet me on the mountain.

It is time to choose

between the Lord and Baal."

Elijah asked for two bulls.

"Call on the name of your god,"

Elijah told the people.

"I will call on the Lord.

The god who answers by fire,

he is God."

The 450 priests of Baal

put one bull on Baal's altar.

The priests called on their god

all day. Nothing happened.

They called louder.

They cut themselves with swords.

Still there was no answer.

Then Elijah fixed God's altar.

He put the bull on the altar

and poured water all around.

"O Lord," prayed Elijah,

"let everyone know that *you*

are God."

The fire of the Lord burned up

the bull, the wood,

the stones, and the soil.

It licked up all the water.

The people fell down and cried,

"The Lord, he is God!"

Then the rain came.

In a Chariot of Fire

from 1 Kings 19 and 2 Kings 2

God told Elijah,

"Go and make Elisha your helper.

Someday,

Elisha will take your place

as my prophet."

Elijah found Elisha.

He was plowing with oxen.

As a sign,

Elijah put his coat around Elisha.

Elisha left his plowing

and became Elijah's helper.

The day came

for Elisha to take Elijah's place.

At the Jordan River,

Elijah rolled up his coat.

He hit the water with his coat,

and the water parted.

Elijah and Elisha

walked across a dry path.

"If you see me as I leave,"

said Elijah, "you will know

that God will bless you."

A chariot of fire took Elijah

into heaven. Elisha saw it!

Elisha tore his clothes in sadness.

Then he rolled up Elijah's coat.

He struck the water in the river

and the water parted.

"The blessing of God is on Elisha,"

the group of prophets said.

They went to meet him

and bowed to him.

A Gulp and a Great City

from the Book of Jonah

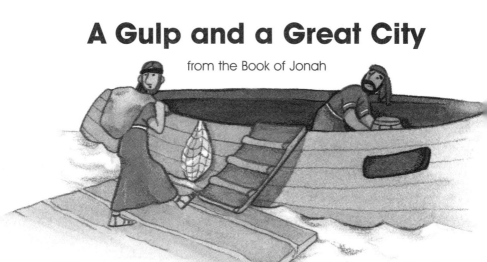

"Go to the great city of Nineveh,"

God said to Jonah.

"Tell the people to change

their wicked ways."

Jonah did not want to preach

to the people of Nineveh.

He ran to the sea

and got on a boat.

God sent a storm on the sea.
The sailors thought the boat
would break.

"I am running away from God,
who made the heavens,
the sea, and the land,"
Jonah told the sailors.
"Throw me into the sea
and the storm will stop."

God sent a great fish

to swallow Jonah.

Inside the fish, Jonah prayed.
After three days, God told the fish
to spit Jonah out onto the land.
"Go to Nineveh," God told Jonah.

This time Jonah obeyed.

"Stop doing evil

or God will destroy your city,"

Jonah told the people.

The people and the king

listened to Jonah and obeyed God.

And God saved their city.

Three Brave Friends

from Daniel 1 and 3

The army of Babylon

fought a long battle

with God's people, the Jews.

Babylon won.

Shadrach, Meshach, and Abednego,

three friends who loved God,

were taken prisoner to Babylon.

The king of Babylon

did not believe

in the one true God.

He tried to build

a god of his own —

a huge golden statue.

"Everyone must bow down
and worship the statue,"
said the king. "If you do not,
you will be thrown
into a fiery furnace!"
Everyone obeyed the king —
but not Shadrach, Meshach,
and Abednego.
"You may have one more chance,"
said the king.
"Never!"
said the three brave friends.
"Our God is able to help us."

Soldiers tied up the three friends
and threw them into the furnace.

Suddenly the king shouted,
"Look! There are *four* in the fire.
And one of them looks like
a son of the gods!"

The three friends were let out

of the fiery furnace.

They were not burned.

"Blessed be the God

of Shadrach, Meshach,

and Abednego!" cried the king.

"No other god

can save in this way!"

Daniel for Dinner?

from Daniel 6

Daniel was the king's

favorite helper.

The king's other helpers

were jealous of Daniel.

They tricked King Darius

into making a new law.

Pray only to the king for 30 days,

or be thrown into the lions' den.

Daniel heard about the new law.

But Daniel loved God.

He kept praying to God,

three times every day.

The king's helpers

spied on Daniel.

Then they ran to tell the king.

"Daniel broke the law!"

said the king's helpers.

King Darius was sad.

"Do what must be done," he said.

Daniel was tossed into a den

of hungry lions.

He could not escape.

And the king could not sleep.

In the morning,

the king hurried to the lions' den.

"Daniel!" he called.

"Has your God rescued you?"

"Yes!" said Daniel.

"The lions did not eat me.

God sent an angel

to shut

their mouths!"

The king set Daniel free.

Then he made

a brand-new law.

Everyone must worship

Daniel's God,

for he is strong

and lives forever!

A Plan and a Party

from the Book of Esther

The king of Persia

chose Esther for his queen.

The king did not know

that Esther was a Jew.

Esther's cousin, Mordecai,

became one of the king's helpers.

But Mordecai would not bow
to Haman, the chief helper.
Haman learned that Mordecai
was a Jew. Haman made a plan.
"A group in your kingdom
does not obey your laws,"
Haman told the king.
"We should destroy them."

"Make a law to do it,"
the king told Haman.
Mordecai heard the news.
He tore his clothes in sadness.
Then he sent a message
to Esther. "Go to the king.
Beg him to help our people."

Esther put on her royal robes.

She stood before the king.

"What can I do for you?"

he asked.

"Come to my feast," Esther said.

"Bring Haman, too.

Then I will tell you what I want."

At the feast, Esther told the king

about the plan to kill her people.

"Who has done this?"

the king asked.

"It is Haman," Esther said.

The king told Esther and Mordecai

to write a new law.

The Jews were allowed

to fight and protect themselves.

Haman was put to death.

And all the Jews in Persia

had a party.

Remember and Obey

from the Book of Nehemiah

Nehemiah was a Jew

who worked

for the king

of Persia.

Nehemiah's brother came to visit.

"The city of Jerusalem

has broken walls

and burned gates," he said.

"The people are sad and afraid."

"Please, God," prayed Nehemiah.

"Please help your people."

"Why are you so sad?"

the king asked Nehemiah.

"My city has broken walls

and burned gates," said Nehemiah.

"The people are sad and afraid."

"You may go and help them,"

said the king.

Nehemiah went to Jerusalem.

"Come, let us fix this wall!"

he called. "God will help us."

Enemies tried to stop the work.

But each day,

half the men worked

and half kept enemies away.

The wall was finished in 52 days.

Then the laws

God gave to Moses

were read out loud.

The people were sad

because they had not obeyed

God's laws. But Nehemiah said,

"This is a happy day,

because now you *want*

to obey God."

The people sang and feasted.

They promised to remember God

and always to obey him.

The Promised One

from Psalms, Isaiah, Micah, and Zechariah

God promised his people

that he would send

a Savior to help them.

God told his promises

to his prophets,

who wrote the promises down.

212

For hundreds of years
before the Savior came,
God's people read the promises
and hoped he would come soon.

A child will be born.
A son will be given.
He will be called
Wonderful Counselor,
Mighty God,
Everlasting Father,
and Prince of Peace.

Isaiah 9

O Bethlehem,
even though you are small,
out of you
will come for me
one who will rule Israel.

Micah 5

His peace will never end.
In his kingdom will be
everything that is right.

Isaiah 9

He will be born
from a virgin.
You will call him Immanuel,
which means
"God with us."

Isaiah 7

He will die
like someone who is evil.
He will be counted with
those who have done
wrong things.
His death will
take away sins.

Isaiah 53

We will look at him
and be full of sadness.
But God will protect him.
Not one of his bones
will be broken.

Zechariah 12, Psalm 34

He will chase away all sadness.
The people who walk in darkness
will see a great light.

Isaiah 9

What's in the
New Testament?

The New Testament tells the rest of the story of God's wonderful plan for us.

When the time was just right, God sent his Son, Jesus, to be the Savior of the world. Jesus showed us what God is like and taught us how to live to please God.

Some leaders of the people hated Jesus and the things he taught. They were jealous of him, too. These people had Jesus killed. But after Jesus died and was buried, God raised him to life again!

After 40 more days on earth, Jesus went back to heaven. But God sent his Holy Spirit to give power to Jesus' disciples. The church began. And everyone who believed in Jesus spread the good news that Jesus is alive!

Jesus promised to come back and take his followers to live with him in heaven someday. He will keep that promise, just as God kept his promise to send us a Savior.

THE NEW TESTAMENT

The Man With No Voice

from Luke 1

Zechariah and his wife, Elizabeth,

had never had a child.

And now they were far too old.

But one day,

Zechariah was in the temple,

burning incense to the Lord.

Then an angel came.

Zechariah was afraid!

But the angel said,

"Don't be afraid, Zechariah.

God has heard your prayer.

Soon you and Elizabeth

will have a son.

You will name

him John."

The angel told Zechariah
more about John.

"He will bring you joy,"
the angel said.

"He will lead many people
back to God.

And he will prepare the way
for the coming of the Lord."

Zechariah was puzzled.

"How do I know
all of this
will come true?"
he asked.

"I am Gabriel," the angel said.

"I stand before God.

He has sent me

to tell you the news about John.

Now you will not be able to talk

until all of this happens,

because you did not believe me."

Outside the temple,

people waited for Zechariah.

When he came out,

he had no voice.

He made signs to the people.

"Surely he has seen a vision!"

the people said.

Mary Meets an Angel

from Luke 1

Young Mary of Nazareth

was engaged to marry Joseph.

But before the wedding day,

the angel Gabriel came.

"Hello, Mary," said the angel.

"The Lord is with you."

What does this mean?

wondered Mary.

"Don't be afraid," the angel said.

"You have found favor with God."

Gabriel had big news for Mary.

"You are going to have
a baby boy," he said.

"You will name him Jesus.

He will be great,

and his kingdom will never end."

"How can this be?" asked Mary.

"I don't have a husband."

"God's Holy Spirit will come
upon you," said the angel.
"That is why the baby
will be called the Son of God.
And your cousin Elizabeth
is having a child,
even though she is old.
Nothing is impossible with God."

"I have always loved God,"
Mary said quietly.
"And I will be his servant.
Let everything happen
just as you have said."
Then the angel left
as quickly
as he had appeared.

His Name Is John

from Luke 1

Mary was eager to tell Elizabeth
the angel's news.

She went to Elizabeth's house
for a visit.

"Elizabeth!" called Mary.

"I am here!"

Elizabeth's baby
jumped inside her,
and God's Spirit filled Elizabeth
with sudden joy.
"You will be the mother
of my Lord!" she told Mary.

How does Elizabeth know about
my baby? wondered Mary.
"My heart is happy," Mary said,
"because God is my Savior."
Mary stayed with Elizabeth
for a few months
and then went home.

Soon Elizabeth's baby was born.

"We will name him John,"

said Elizabeth.

"What?" said her friends.

"You are not naming him

Zechariah, like his father?"

They asked Zechariah,

"What would you like to name

this child?"

On a tablet, Zechariah wrote,

"His name is John."

At that moment,
Zechariah could talk again,
and he began to praise God.
Everyone was amazed.
"What will this baby be
when he is grown?"
asked people everywhere.

One Night in Bethlehem

from Luke 2

"The king wants to know
how many people
are in his kingdom,"
Joseph told Mary.
"We must go to my hometown
and be counted."
Mary patted her large middle.
"Bethlehem is far away, Joseph,"
she sighed.
"And the baby is due
any day now."

238

"Please don't worry,"

Joseph told Mary.

"God will watch over us."

239

The trip to Bethlehem
was long and dusty.
And Bethlehem was crowded.
Joseph tried to find a room
where they could stay.
"Sorry," said the innkeeper.
"Every room here is full."

But Mary and Joseph

found a warm, clean stable.

And there Mary's baby was born.

The baby was a boy, Jesus,

just as God's angel had said!

Mary wrapped her newborn baby
in cloths to keep him warm.
Tenderly she laid him
in his first bed —
a simple feeding box
under the stars,
one night in Bethlehem.

Good News of Great Joy

from Luke 2

On the hills near Bethlehem,
shepherds watched their sheep.
Suddenly the night was bright!
And standing near the shepherds
was an angel of the Lord.

244

The shepherds were afraid!
But the angel said,
"Calm down, for I have come
with good news of great joy!
Today in Bethlehem
a Savior has been born to you.
Christ the Lord has come!"

"You may go to see him,"
the angel told the shepherds.
"This will be a sign for you.
You will find the baby
wrapped in cloths
and lying in a feeding box."

Then there were angels

all around,

praising God and saying,

"Glory to God in the highest!

And peace to his people

on earth!"

When the angels were gone,

the shepherds said,

"Let's go to Bethlehem!"

They hurried into town

and found Mary and Joseph

and the baby, just as the angel

had said.

Then the shepherds went back
to their sheep,
praising God all the way.

Follow That Star!

from Matthew 2

Wise men from the east

came to Jerusalem.

"Where is the child who was born

king of the Jews?" they asked.

"We saw his star in the east.

We have come to worship him."

King Herod was angry.

He wanted to be the only king!

He called the Jewish leaders.

"Tell me where the Christ

will be born," he said.

"In Bethlehem," they told him,

"just as the prophet wrote."

"Go to Bethlehem,"

Herod told the wise men.

"Look for the child there.

When you find him,

come and tell me.

I want to worship him, too."

But King Herod was lying.

He did not want

to worship the baby.

He wanted to have him killed.

The wise men left for Bethlehem.

"Look!" they said.

"There is the star again."

They followed the star

until it stopped

right over the house

where Jesus was.

The wise men went inside.

They saw Jesus

with Mary, his mother.

They bowed down

to worship him

and gave him precious gifts.

That night in a dream,
God sent a warning
to the wise men.
"Do not go back
to King Herod," God said.
So the wise men went home
by a different road.

Taller and Wiser

from Luke 2

When Jesus was 12,

he went with Mary and Joseph

to the Passover feast in Jerusalem.

Passover was a time to remember

how God had saved his people

from slavery in Egypt.

When the feast was over,

Mary and Joseph

and others from their town

began the trip home.

They thought Jesus was with them.

At the end of the day, Mary asked,

"Where is Jesus?" No one knew.

Mary and Joseph went back
to Jerusalem.
They looked up and down
the streets of the city.
They found Jesus at the temple,
talking with the teachers.
Everyone who listened
was surprised.
Jesus understood so much
about God and his ways!
"Son," said Mary,
"why have you made us
search for you?"

"Why were you looking for me?"
asked Jesus.

"Didn't you know I had to be
in my Father's house?"
Then Jesus went home
with Mary and Joseph
and always obeyed them.

Mary often thought about
all these things.
And Jesus kept on growing
taller and wiser,
pleasing all who knew him
and pleasing God.

The Right Thing to Do

from Matthew 3, Mark 1, and Luke 3

When John grew up,

he preached to God's people.

"Get ready!" he told them.

"Change how you live.

The kingdom of heaven

is coming soon."

262

At the Jordan River,

many people said,

"John, we are sorry

we have not obeyed God."

Then John baptized them

in the river.

Jesus came to John
to be baptized.
But John knew
that Jesus had never sinned.
"I need to be baptized
by *you*," John said.
"Why do you come to me?"

"It is important to baptize me,"
Jesus said.

"It is the right thing to do."

So John baptized Jesus.

When Jesus came up
from the water,
heaven opened.
The Spirit of God
came down like a dove
and landed on Jesus.
Then a voice came
from heaven.
"You are my Son,"
said the voice.
"I love you,
and I am very pleased
with you."

Jesus' Team of 12

from Matthew 4, Mark 1 and 3, Luke 5 and 6, and John 1

Two brothers, Peter and Andrew,

washed their fishing nets.

Jesus got into Peter's boat.

"Go out to deep water," Jesus said.

"Put your nets into the water

so you can catch some fish."

"Teacher," said Peter,

"we fished all night.

We could not catch *any* fish."

But Peter obeyed Jesus

and put the nets in the water.

Suddenly, the nets began to break.

They were full of fish!

"Come and help us!"

called Peter and Andrew

to James and John in another boat.

Soon both boats were so full

of fish that they began to sink.

Then Peter knew

that Jesus was from God.

"Don't be afraid," said Jesus.

"Follow me. From now on,

you will catch people, not fish."

Peter and Andrew
left everything
and followed Jesus.
So did James
and John.

And later Jesus also called Philip,

Bartholomew, Matthew, Thomas,

another James, Thaddaeus,

Simon the Zealot, and Judas

to be with him

on his team of 12.

Inside and Out

from Matthew 9, Mark 2, and Luke 5

Jesus was teaching in a house.

A crowd of people

filled the house to hear him.

Then four friends came,

carrying a man

274

who could not move.

"This crowd is too big,"

the four men said.

So they took the man on his mat

up on the roof.

The four men made a hole
in the roof. They lowered their
friend down into the house,
right in front of Jesus.

Jesus saw that the four men
had great faith.
"Your sins are forgiven,"
Jesus told the man on the mat.

The teachers of the law

were saying to themselves,

Who does Jesus think he is?

Only God can forgive sins!

Jesus knew what the teachers
were thinking. He asked them,
"Is it easier to forgive sins
or to say rise and walk?"
Then Jesus told the man
on the mat, "Stand up.
Take your mat and go home."

The man jumped up.

He picked up his mat

and walked out of the house

praising God.

Everyone was amazed.

Jesus had healed the man

on the mat — inside and out!

Jesus the Teacher

from Matthew 5 — 7 and Luke 6

A huge crowd of people
gathered on a grassy hillside.
They had come to see Jesus.
Jesus sat down
and began to teach them.

"Happy are the humble,"
Jesus said.

"Heaven belongs to them.

Whoever is sad will find comfort.

Whoever loves mercy and peace

pleases God."

Jesus looked into the faces

of the crowd.

"Love your enemies," he said.

"Forgive those

who do wrong to you."

Jesus also taught about money.

"Don't worry about getting rich

here on earth," Jesus said.

"Live to please God.

Someday he will reward you

in heaven.

Pray always," said Jesus.

"Seek and you will find."

Then Jesus told a story.

"Everyone who hears me today

and obeys me is like a wise man

who built his house on rock,"

he said.

"When the rain and wind came,

that house stood strong."

"But a foolish man built his house on soft sand," said Jesus.

"When the rain and wind came, his house fell down with a crash. Anyone who doesn't listen to me is like that foolish man."

Just Say the Word

from Matthew 8 and Luke 7

A Roman soldier had

a servant who was dying.

The soldier heard about Jesus.

So he sent some Jewish leaders

to ask Jesus for help.

The leaders found Jesus.

"Please come and heal
the servant of this soldier.
He has been good to us."

"I will come," said Jesus.

Soon Jesus and the Jewish leaders were close to the soldier's house. The soldier sent out some friends with a message for Jesus.

This was the soldier's message:
"I am not good enough
to have you in my house.
Just say my servant is healed
and he will be healed."

Jesus turned to the people

following him.

"This Roman soldier

has very great faith,"

he said.

Then Jesus said

to the soldier's friends,

"Go back to the house.

What you have asked

will be done."

The soldier's friends

went back to the house.

They opened the door

and saw the soldier.

And next to him was his servant,

who was completely well!

Wild Winds and Waves Obey

from Matthew 8, Mark 4, and Luke 8

Jesus was tired.

All day long he had been teaching

from a boat on the lake.

When evening came,

Jesus said to his disciples,

"Let's go over to the other side

of the lake."

In the back of the boat,

Jesus went to sleep.

Then a wild storm began.
The wind howled, and waves
came over the sides of the boat.
"We are in danger!"
cried the disciples.

The disciples woke up Jesus.

"Teacher, Teacher, save us!"

they cried.

"Don't you care

that we are going to drown?"

Jesus got up.

He turned to the roaring waters.

"Quiet!" he said. "Be still!"

The wind went away.

The waves were still.

Jesus said to his disciples,

"Why are you so afraid?

Where is your faith?"

"What kind of man is this?"

the disciples asked each other.

"Even the wind

and the waves

obey him!"

296

Enough for Everyone

from Matthew 14, Mark 6, Luke 9, and John 6

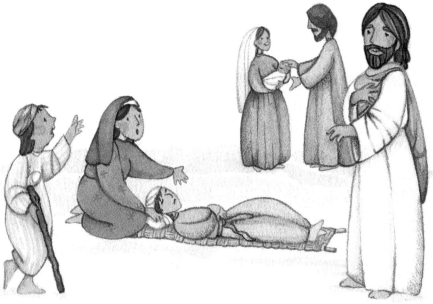

Jesus and his disciples were busy.

"Take away my sickness,"

said a man.

"Heal my son," said a woman.

Jesus and his helpers did not rest.

"Get into this boat," said Jesus.

"We will go to a quiet place

on the other side of the lake."

The people ran around the lake

to meet Jesus there.

But Jesus was not angry.

"Bring the sick to me," he said.

Late in the afternoon,

Jesus' disciples said,

"Send the people to town

for food."

"No," said Jesus.

"We will feed them."

Andrew found a boy

with five loaves of bread

and two small fish.

"But that is not enough

to feed a crowd," said Andrew.

"Tell the people to sit

on the grass," said Jesus.

Jesus thanked God for the food.

He broke the bread and fish
into pieces.

"Give the food to all the people,"
Jesus told the disciples.

Five thousand men,

plus women and children,

had enough to eat.

The leftovers filled 12 baskets.

"Jesus must come from God,"

the people said.

Then Jesus quietly went up

the mountainside to pray.

Peter Takes a Walk

from Matthew 14, Mark 6, and John 6

"Take the boat

to the other side of the lake,"

Jesus told his disciples.

"I will meet you later."

Jesus went up into the hills

to pray.

The disciples obeyed Jesus.

But a mighty wind began to blow.

It blew against the boat

as the disciples tried to row.

Jesus prayed a long time.

Then he went down to the shore

and began to walk

across the water toward the boat.

The disciples thought
they were seeing a ghost.
"It is I," called Jesus.
"Don't be afraid!"
But Peter called out,
"Lord, if it is really you,
tell me to come and meet you."
"Come!" said Jesus.

Peter stepped out of the boat
and began to walk to Jesus
on the water.
But the wind and waves
pushed and pulled at him.
Peter was afraid,
and he began to sink.
"Lord, save me!" he cried.
Jesus reached out to Peter
and helped him back into the boat.

"Why did you begin to doubt?"
said Jesus.

Jesus got into the boat, too.

And the wind stopped!

Jesus' disciples worshiped him
in the boat.

Now I See

from John 9

Jesus saw a man

who had been born blind.

The disciples asked Jesus,

"Is this man blind

because he sinned

or because his parents sinned?"

"No," said Jesus.

"It is so that God's power

can be shown in him."

Jesus spit on the ground

and made some mud.

He put the mud

on the blind man's eyes.

"Now go wash

in the pool of Siloam,"

Jesus told the man.

The blind man did

what Jesus told him.

And he could see!

"Isn't this the man

who was blind from birth?"

said the neighbors.

"How did this happen?"
asked the teachers.
"Truly the one who healed me
is from God," said the happy man.
But the teachers did not want
to believe it.

Jesus found the man again.

"Do you believe

in the Son of Man?" asked Jesus.

"Who is he?" said the man.

Jesus smiled.

"You have seen him now,

and he is the one talking to you."

"Lord, I do believe in you!"

cried the happy man.

"I came into this world

so that many will believe,"

said Jesus.

A Neighbor Shows Kindness

from Luke 10

A teacher of the Jewish law

came to Jesus with a question.

"God's law tells me to love God

with all my heart, my soul,

my strength, and my mind.

And to love my neighbor

as myself.

But who is my neighbor?"

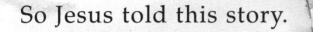

So Jesus told this story.

A man was traveling

down a rough and rocky road.

Then robbers grabbed him,

took his clothes, and beat him.

They left him lying on the road.

317

A priest came along the road.

He saw the hurt man.

But he went by on the other side.

A temple worker

came along the road.

He saw the hurt man, too.

But he went by on the other side.

A man from Samaria
came along the road.
Jews did not like Samaritans.
But this Samaritan stopped.
He cleaned the hurt man's wounds
and put on bandages.
Then he took the man
to an inn.

The Samaritan had to leave

the next day.

But he used his own money

to pay the innkeeper.

"Look after this man,"

he said to the innkeeper.

"If you need more money,

I will give it to you

when I come back."

Then Jesus asked
the teacher of the law,
"Which of the three travelers
was a neighbor to the hurt man?"
"The one who helped him,"
said the teacher of the law.
Jesus said, "Go and do the same."

Teach Us to Pray

from Matthew 6 and Luke 11

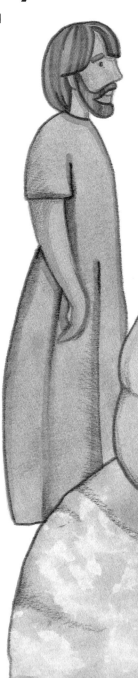

Jesus was praying.

When he was done,

one of his disciples said,

"Lord, please teach us

to pray."

Jesus gave his disciples

a prayer for an example.

322

"When you pray," said Jesus, "pray like this."

Our Father in heaven,
your name will always be
great and holy.

Be our king!
Set up your heavenly kingdom
here on earth.

Give us our food
for today.

Forgive our sins.
And help us forgive others
who have done wrong
to us.

Jesus finished the example prayer with these words.

Lead us away from wanting to do wrong things. Free us from the evil one.

Because the kingdom

is yours,

with power

and glory forever.

Amen.

Lost and Found

from Luke 15

Jesus told this story.

A man's younger son

asked for his share

of the family money.

Then he left home.

The young man
wasted all his money.
When his money was gone,
no one would give him anything.
The only job he could find
was feeding pigs.
He was so hungry
that even the pigs' food
looked good to him.

"My father's servants
have food to eat," said the son.
"I will go back to my father
and be one of his servants."
While the young man
was still a long way from home,
his father saw him.

The father ran to his son
and hugged him.

"Quick! Give him the best robe,"
the father told his servants.

"Put a ring on his finger,
and sandals on his feet.

Prepare for a party!

My son has come home!"

Then the young man's brother

came in from the fields.

"Come to the party,"

the father said.

"No," said the brother.

"You have never given

a party for *me*."

"But you are always with me,"

said the father,

"and everything I have is yours.

We had to have a party,

because your brother,

who was lost, has been found!"

Lazarus Lives Again

from John 11

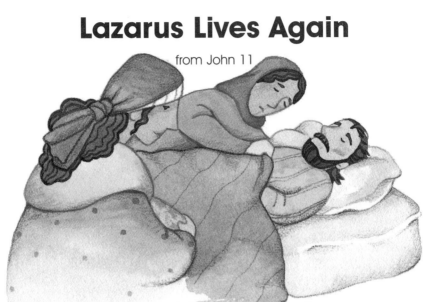

Lazarus, who lived in Bethany,

was very sick.

Mary and Martha, his sisters,

sent someone to tell Jesus,

"Your friend Lazarus is sick."

But Jesus stayed where he was

for two more days.

When Jesus came to Bethany,

Lazarus was dead.

"Lord," said Martha,

"if you had been here,

my brother would not have died."

"Your brother will live again,"
said Jesus.

"I am the resurrection and the life.
He who believes in me will live."

"I believe you are the Son of God,"
said Martha.

Then Mary came to Jesus
and fell at his feet and said,
"Lord, if you had been here,
my brother would not have died."
Mary and the friends with her
were crying.

337

Jesus was very sad.

"Where have you laid Lazarus?"

he asked.

They showed him the place.

Jesus cried. Then Jesus said,

"Take away the stone."

He called out in a loud voice,

"Lazarus, come out!"

And Lazarus came out, alive.

"Take off the grave clothes,"

Jesus said,

"and let him go."

One Thankful Man

from Luke 17

Jesus came near a village between Samaria and Galilee. There he heard a loud cry, "Master, please help us!"

Jesus saw ten men

standing by themselves.

They had a terrible skin disease

called leprosy.

No one wanted them around.

341

But Jesus was not afraid
of the sick men.
He wanted to help them.
"Go show yourselves
to the village priests,"
Jesus told them.

The ten men obeyed Jesus.
And as they were walking
to find the priests,
suddenly their sores disappeared!

One of the men ran back to Jesus.

He bowed down at Jesus' feet.

"Oh, thank you, Master!"

he cried.

And he was a Samaritan,

not a Jew like Jesus

and the disciples.

Jesus looked around.

"Where are the others?" he said.

"Did I not heal *ten* men?

Is this Samaritan the only one

who gives praise to God?"

Then Jesus smiled at the man

and said, "Get up and go now.

You were healed

because you believed."

Let the Children Come

from Matthew 19, Mark 10, and Luke 18

Some mothers and fathers

came to Jesus.

They carried babies in their arms.

They held their boys and girls

by the hand.

346

"We want Jesus
to pray for our children,"
the mothers and fathers said.
"We want Jesus
to give them his blessing."

But Jesus' disciples tried to stop

the mothers and the fathers.

"Get back!" they said.

"Can't you see that Jesus is busy?

He does not have time

for children!"

Jesus heard his disciples.
He reached out his arms
and called to the children.
"Let the children come to me,"
he said. "Don't stop them."

Jesus told his disciples,

"The kingdom of God

belongs to children like these!

Everyone needs

the simple faith of a child

to enter the kingdom."

Jesus hugged the boys and girls.

He held the babies.

And to the delight

of the mothers and fathers,

Jesus laid his hands

on all the children

and blessed them.

Big News for a Little Man

from Luke 19

Zaccheus the tax collector

felt squished.

He wanted to see Jesus.

But no one liked a tax collector.

No one would let

Zaccheus through

to the front of the line.

Then Zaccheus

had an idea.

He climbed a tree!

"Hello, Zaccheus,"

said a gentle voice.

Zaccheus looked down.

The voice belonged to Jesus!

353

"Come down quickly," said Jesus.

"I must stay at your house today."

"At *my* house?" said Zaccheus.

"Of course," said Jesus.

Zaccheus was happy.

He welcomed Jesus to his house.

People in the crowd were saying,

"Zaccheus is a bad man!

Jesus has gone to the house

of a liar and a thief!"

"What the people say is true,"

Zaccheus told Jesus.

"I have cheated people.

But I am sorry."

"I know," said Jesus.

"That is why I came."

Zaccheus decided

to make things right.

"I will share with the poor,"

he said.

"And I will pay back

everyone I cheated.

I will give back

extra money besides."

Jesus was pleased.

"This is a good-news day,"

he said.

Praise to the King of Kings!

from Matthew 21, Mark 11, Luke 19, and John 12

Jesus and his disciples

came to a village near Jerusalem.

"Go into the village,"

Jesus said to two disciples.

"You will see a donkey

and her colt.

Bring the colt to me."

The disciples did what Jesus said.

Some people asked,

"Why are you taking that colt?"

"The Lord needs it,"

the disciples said.

"He will send it back later."

The disciples brought the colt

to Jesus.

They spread their coats

on the colt's back.

Jesus sat on the colt.

A large crowd gathered.

Some spread their coats

on the road in front of Jesus.

Others spread palm branches

from the fields along the road.

Jesus rode toward Jerusalem.

Some of the people

in the crowd

went ahead of Jesus.

Some of the people followed.

Everyone shouted,

"Blessed is the one

who comes in the name

of the Lord!

Blessed is the one

who comes from the family

of David!"

Jesus entered Jerusalem
like a gentle king.

Remember Me

from Matthew 26, Mark 14, Luke 22,
John 13, and 1 Corinthians 11

On the night of Passover,

Jesus and his disciples

met in an upper room.

364

Jesus wrapped a towel
around his waist.
Then he washed
his disciples' feet.

"I served you
by washing your feet,"
said Jesus.
"You also must serve others."

During the meal, Jesus took bread.

He said a prayer of thanks.

He broke the bread

and gave it to his disciples.

"This is my body," Jesus said.

"My body will be broken for you.

Then I want you to break bread

together and

remember me."

Jesus took a cup.

He said a prayer of thanks

and gave the cup to his disciples.

"This cup is a new promise,"

he said. "When I die,

my blood will be poured out

for you. Then I want you

to drink the cup together

and remember me."

Jesus and the disciples
sang a hymn together
before they left
the upper room.

A Sad, Dark Night

from Matthew 26, Mark 14, Luke 22, and John 18

Jesus and his disciples

went to a garden.

"Sit here while I pray," he said.

Jesus walked ahead.

He took Peter, James, and John.

"My soul is full of sadness," Jesus said. "Stay here and keep watch." He walked a little farther. "Father, you can do anything," he prayed. "Take this suffering away. But do what you want, not what I want."

An angel came to Jesus

to help him.

Three times Jesus prayed.

Each time when he went back

to Peter, James, and John,

they were asleep. "Peter," he said,

"stay awake and pray."

When Jesus came back
the third time, he said,
"Are you still sleeping?
The hour has come."
Soldiers came into the garden.
They grabbed Jesus.

"I know this must happen,"
Jesus said.

"What the prophets wrote about
must come true."

So the soldiers took Jesus away.

And Jesus' disciples were afraid

King of a Different Kingdom

from Matthew 27, Mark 15, Luke 23, and John 19

A judgment was made.

Jesus would have to die

on a cross!

Soldiers put a purple robe on him.

They put a crown of thorns

on his head.

Making fun of him, they said,

"Here is the king."

Then Jesus had to carry

a heavy wooden cross

to a hill called Calvary.

A crowd followed him.

On the cross, Jesus said,
"Father, forgive them.
They do not know
what they are doing."

378

Two robbers hung on crosses
beside Jesus.

"Jesus, remember me
when you are king," said one.

"Today you will be with me
in my heavenly kingdom,"
Jesus told him.

Then darkness covered
the whole earth.

Jesus called out
in a loud voice,

"Father, I give myself to you!"
And Jesus died.

At that moment,

the temple curtain in Jerusalem

ripped in half.

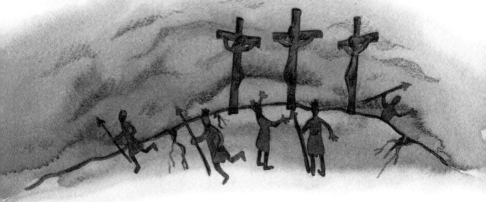

The earth shook and rocks split.

The soldiers at the cross said,

"Surely he was the Son of God!"

A rich man named Joseph

wrapped Jesus' body

in clean linen cloths.

He put the body into a new tomb.

Then a big, heavy stone

was rolled in front of the tomb

to close it tight.

Could It Be True?

from Matthew 28, Mark 16, Luke 24, and John 20

It was the first day of the week.

The sun was coming up.

Mary Magdalene

and the other women

went to Jesus' tomb.

They carried sweet-smelling spices

to place around Jesus' body.

"How will we get into the tomb?"

asked one of the women.

"Who will roll the stone away?"

382

But when the women got there,

the stone was rolled away already!

An angel from God had done it.

The women walked into the tomb.

Jesus' body was gone!

Mary ran to tell Peter and John.

Then two angels came
to the other women.

"Don't be afraid," the angels said.

"You are looking for Jesus.

But he is not here. He has risen!"

The women hurried away

to tell the disciples.

After the women were gone,

Peter and John came running.

The tomb was empty,

just as Mary had said!

Then John

believed that

Jesus was alive

again.

But Peter

wondered.

It Is True!

from Luke 24 and John 20

Mary Magdalene went back

to the empty tomb.

She was crying.

What had happened to Jesus?

"Why are you crying?"

she heard someone ask.

Mary thought it was the gardener.

Then Mary heard her name.

The one talking to her was Jesus!

"Teacher!" cried Mary.

Mary ran to tell the disciples

that she had seen the Lord.

The other women were
on their way to tell the disciples
what the angels had said.
Suddenly, they met Jesus!
"Don't be afraid," he told them.
"Go and tell my disciples
to go to Galilee," Jesus said.
"They will see me there."
The women hurried
to find the disciples.

That evening,

all the disciples except Thomas

were together in a locked room.

Suddenly Jesus was with them.

"Peace be with you!" Jesus said.

The disciples were filled with joy.

And a week later,

Thomas saw Jesus, too.

"My Lord and my God!"

said Thomas.

Parting Promises

from Matthew 28, Luke 24, and Acts 1

Jesus stayed on earth

for 40 days after he arose.

On a hill in Galilee,

Jesus told the disciples,

"You will receive power.

Go to all the nations.

394

Make disciples everywhere.

Baptize them in the name

of the Father, Son, and Holy Spirit.

Teach them to obey

everything I have taught you.

I will be with you always."

On his last day on earth,

Jesus led the disciples

to the Mount of Olives.

He lifted his hands

to bless the disciples.

While he was blessing them,

Jesus went up into heaven.

The disciples kept looking up

until he was hidden by a cloud.

Then two men dressed in white

stood beside the disciples.

"Why are you looking

into the sky?" they asked.

"Jesus has been taken from you.

But he will come back

just as you have seen him go."

Then the disciples
went back to Jerusalem
with great joy.
And they stayed in the temple,
praising God.

The Very First Church

from Acts 2

On the Jewish holiday
called Pentecost,
the disciples met together
in a house in Jerusalem.
A sound like a strong wind
suddenly filled the house.

400

Then what looked like tongues

of fire rested on the disciples.

God's Holy Spirit

filled the disciples.

They began to speak

in other languages.

People heard the noise
and gathered around the house.
"What's going on?" they asked.
Everyone could hear
his own language being spoken,
even the people from other lands!

Peter said, "Listen!

What the prophet Joel

wrote about is happening today.

God says, I will pour out

my Spirit upon all people.

And everyone who trusts

in the Lord will be saved."

"Jesus was killed," said Peter.

"But God made him alive again.

We have seen him!

He is in heaven now.

Jesus is the Christ,

the one God promised to send."

The crowd gasped.

"What shall we do?" they asked.

"Repent," said Peter.

"Be baptized for the forgiveness

of your sins.

And you will receive

the gift of the Holy Spirit."

Three thousand people

believed in Jesus

and were baptized that day!

Jumping for Joy

from Acts 3

Peter and John

went to the temple to pray.

At the temple gate sat a man

who could not walk.

Every day, his friends carried him

to the gate to sit and beg.

The man asked Peter and John
for money.
"I have no money," said Peter.
"But I have something else.
In the name of Jesus,
rise and walk!"

Peter grabbed the man's hand

and began to help him up.

Right then the man was healed.

He jumped to his feet

and began to walk.

He went into the temple

courtyard with Peter and John,

walking and jumping

and praising God.

People came running
to see the man. "This is the one
who used to beg," they said.
"What has happened to him?"
"Don't stare at *us*," said Peter.
"We did not heal this man."

"This man was healed

by the power of Jesus," said Peter.

"Jesus was killed on the cross.

But God made him alive again,

and we have seen him!

He is with God in heaven now,

just as the prophets said."

Saul Sees the Light

from Acts 9

Saul did not want

anyone to believe in Jesus.

He went to the high priest.

"Let me arrest any believers

I find in Damascus," Saul said.

Then Saul set out for Damascus.

But on the way there, suddenly

a light from heaven flashed.

Saul fell to the ground.

He heard a voice say, "Saul, Saul,

why are you hurting me so?"

"Who are you, Lord?" asked Saul.

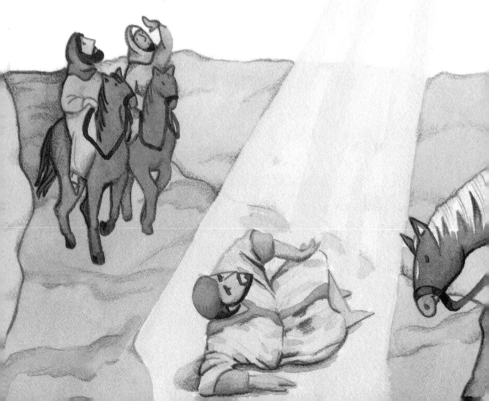

"I am Jesus," said the voice.

"Get up now and go into the city.

Someone will tell you

what to do."

When Saul got up, he was blind.

His friends led him into the city.

God sent a man named Ananias
to the house where Saul was.
Ananias laid his hands on Saul.
"The Lord Jesus sent me
so you can see again
and be filled with the Holy Spirit."

Then Saul could see again.

He got up

and was baptized

as a new believer

in Jesus.

Saul began to preach
to the Jews in Damascus.
"Jesus is truly God's Son,"
he told them.
"Isn't this the man
who arrests believers?"
the Jews asked each other.
"What has happened to him?"

Timothy Joins the Journey

from Acts 15 and 16 and 2 Timothy 1

Saul became known as Paul.

Paul traveled from place

to place, preaching about Jesus.

In each town,

the new believers met together

as a church.

Paul wanted to see

if the new churches were growing.

So Paul and his friend Silas

traveled to Galatia.

There they stopped

at a city called Lystra.

They visited a young believer

named Timothy.

Timothy's mother

and his grandmother

were believers, too.

Paul had a question for Timothy.

"We are traveling

to visit the new churches,"

Paul told him.

"Will you come with us?"

Timothy was happy

to join the journey.

So Paul, Silas, and Timothy

traveled together

to cheer the churches

and tell others about Jesus.

Paul learned to love

young Timothy

like a son.

And the churches

grew stronger in faith,

with new believers

added every day.

422

The Night the Prison Shook

from Acts 16

Paul and Silas went to Philippi.

They preached about Jesus.

But they were arrested

by angry people who didn't want

to hear about Jesus.

424

"Beat them," said the judges.

"Put them in prison.

And don't let them escape!"

The prison guard put chains

on Paul and Silas.

He put their feet in stocks.

But at midnight Paul and Silas

were singing and praying out loud.

The other prisoners heard them.

Suddenly, an earthquake

shook the prison.

All the doors flew open.

Everyone's

chains

broke loose.

The guard woke up.

He was afraid.

Had his prisoners escaped?

"Don't worry!" shouted Paul.

"We are all here."

"What must I do to be saved?"
asked the thankful guard.
"Believe in the Lord Jesus,"
said Paul and Silas. "He will
save you and your whole family."

428

Paul told the guard

and his family more about Jesus.

The guard washed

Paul and Silas's wounds.

Then he and his family

were baptized. He was filled

with joy!

Come Quickly, Lord Jesus!

from Revelation

John was arrested

for teaching about Jesus.

He was sent to live

on an island called Patmos.

God gave John visions

while he was

on the island.

In one vision, John saw Jesus.

"Write on a scroll what you see,"

Jesus told him.

"Send it to the churches."

John also saw heaven.

There he saw angels

around God's throne

and every creature

in heaven and earth

singing praise to God and Jesus.

Out of heaven came a new city,

made of gold and precious gems.

A crystal-clear river

flowed through the city,

and God's throne was there.

"There is no sun or moon,"

wrote John.

"The glory of God gives it light."

In the new city,

John heard a loud voice

from God's throne.

"Now God will live here

with his people.

He will wipe every tear

from their eyes.

There will be no more death

or crying or pain."

"I am coming soon,"

Jesus told John.

Come quickly, Lord Jesus!

How Did We Get the Bible?

The Bible is God's Word — God's message to us. But how did we get the Bible?

There are 66 different books in the Bible, but they all are part of one story, the story of God's people. The 66 books were written by about 40 different writers. Not every book of the Bible was written at the same time. But God guided all the writers. So we can be sure that what the Bible says is exactly what God wants us to know!

Most of the books in the Bible were written on scrolls made of *papyrus*. Thin strips of the papyrus plant were placed together into the shape of a long page. The pieces dried in the sun and stuck together. Then the long page was rolled up into a *scroll*.

The Bible scrolls were saved for many years. They also were copied onto other scrolls (and later into books) so that more people could read what was written.

By about A.D. 500, church leaders had put all 66 books together and called it the Bible. The word "Bible" comes from the Greek word that means "book."

But the Bible still wasn't ready for *you* to read. That's because it wasn't written in English. Some of the books were written in the Hebrew language, and others were written in Greek or Aramaic. First the Bible was translated into Latin. Then, about 600 years ago, in 1382, the Bible was translated into English. But every copy had to be made by hand. The first printed English Bible was not published until around 1455.

Of course, not everyone in the world speaks English. So the Bible has been translated into other languages, too. There's a Spanish Bible, a French Bible, a Chinese Bible, and a Russian Bible, just to name a few. But some groups of people in the world still do not have the Bible in their own language.

How exciting to know that the Bible is a message from God, for us! He has watched over this special book from the beginning and kept it safe so that everyone can read it—everyone including you!

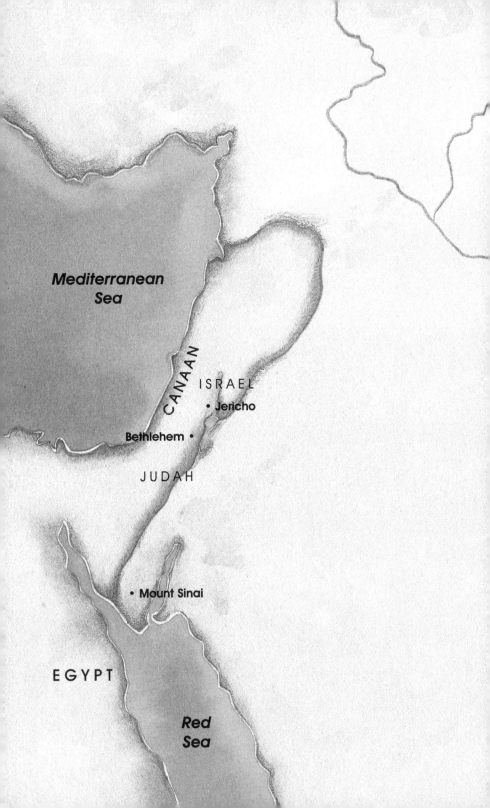

Mediterranean Sea

C A N A A N

I S R A E L

• Jericho

Bethlehem •

J U D A H

• Mount Sinai

E G Y P T

Red Sea

Nineveh

Babylon

Tigris River

PERSIA

Euphrates River

Ur

Persian
Gulf

Old
Testament
Map

Can You Find . . . ?

Look on the Old and New Testament maps on pages 438-39 and 441. Can you find . . .

- **Ur**, where Abraham began his long journey when God told him to leave his home?
- **Egypt**, where the Hebrews were slaves?
- **Mount Sinai**, where Moses was given the ten commandments?
- **Jericho**, where the walls fell down?
- **Nineveh**, where Jonah preached for God?
- **Babylon**, where God saved Shadrach, Meshach, and Abednego from the fiery flames?
- **Nazareth**, the hometown of Mary and Joseph?
- **Bethlehem**, where Jesus was born?
- The **Jordan River**, where Jesus was baptized?
- The **Sea of Galilee**, where Jesus stopped a storm?
- **Bethsaida**, where Jesus fed more than 5,000 hungry people?
- **Bethany**, where Jesus brought Lazarus back to life?
- **Jerusalem**, where Jesus died and was buried and was raised to life again?
- **Damascus**, where Saul became a believer in Jesus?

Damascus

Mediterranean Sea

Capernaum •   • Bethsaida

Sea of Galilee

Nazareth •

GALILEE

SAMARIA

Jordan River

Bethany
Jerusalem •   •
Bethlehem •

JUDEA

Dead Sea

New Testament Map

When Did It Happen?

Noah
Inside the ark **1 year and 17 days**

Adam and Eve
Creation **6 days**

Abraham
Moves to Canaan
2091 B.C.

B.C. means "before Christ." **A.D.** means an event happened after Jesus was born. (**A.D.** stands for "in the year of our Lord" in Latin — "anno domini.") After this way of counting years was invented, a mistake was found. This is why Jesus' birth is listed as about 4 B.C.

Jacob
Travels to Haran **1929** B.C.

Ruth
Her son Obed born **1075** B.C.

Joshua
Defeats city of Jericho
1406 B.C.

Moses
Leads Hebrews out of Egypt
1446 B.C.
The ten commandments
1445 B.C.

Joseph
Sold into slavery **1898** B.C.
Rules in Egypt **1885** B.C.

Samuel
Prophet in Israel 1063 B.C.

Daniel
Prophet in Babylon
605 B.C.

David
King of Israel
1010-970 B.C.

Jonah
Prophet in Israel
780-760 B.C.

Solomon
King of Israel 970-931 B.C.

Elijah
Prophet in Israel 865-835 B.C.

Jesus
Birth about 4 B.C.

Baptized A.D. 26

Crucified A.D. 30

John
Sent to Patmos
A.D. 95

Raised to life
on the third day

Paul
Becomes a believer
A.D. 34

Went back to heaven
after 40 days on earth

The church begins
Pentecost A.D. 30

What Does It Mean?

altar
A special table, sometimes made of stones, used to burn gifts for God as a way of showing that people were sorry for their sins.

anoint
Pouring oil over a person's head to show that God had chosen him for a special job.

Christ
A Greek word that means "God's chosen one." The Hebrew word "Messiah" means the same thing.

disciple
The 12 men Jesus chose to be with him and learn from him. Also, anyone who believes that Jesus is the Son of God and follows his teachings.

faith
Being sure about something. A person with faith in Jesus is sure that Jesus is God's Son. Faith also means believing that what God says is true.

idol
Anything people worship instead of God.

incense
Special perfume that was burned in the temple.

priest
A special temple worker who helped the people burn their gifts to God on the altar.

prophet
Someone who gives people messages from God.

resurrection
To come back to life after being dead.

Savior
Someone who saves people from danger. Jesus saved us from being punished for our sins. He is the Savior God promised to send. The name Jesus means "Savior."

sin
Things people do, think, or say that are wrong because they are not what God wants.

temple
A building for worship. King Solomon built a temple in Jerusalem.

thresh
A way to get grains of wheat from the cut stalks.

vision
Something like a dream that could come to a person when he was awake or asleep. God sometimes gave people visions to teach them or to tell them something that was going to happen.

The People Who Created
The Young Reader's Bible

Bonnie Bruno has spent much of her adult life working with children in Sunday school, children's church, VBS, and as a tutor in elementary schools. She has written Sunday school curriculum and contributed to a variety of Christian magazines. Now a columnist for *Newsday*, Bonnie lives in Albany, Oregon, where she is currently working on her ninth book.

Carol Reinsma is a writer for children and a substitute teacher. She has authored five children's stories with Standard and has completed three devotional books for children. Carol lives in Colorado Springs, Colorado, where she also enjoys writing and directing plays for her congregation's summer program.

Jenifer Schneider, illustrator, lives in Dayton, Ohio. The opportunity to create the artwork for *The Young Reader's Bible* came at a challenging time in her life. She chose to take on the project as a thank-you to God for a talent that has given her much joy.

With Bonnie, Carol, and Jenifer, all of us at Standard Publishing have truly enjoyed creating this book. Our prayer is that *The Young Reader's Bible* will help children everywhere begin a lifetime adventure of reading God's Word. And may we all hide God's Word in our hearts and obey it always!